SLIMY SLUGS
AND GRUBBY BUGS

LEVEL **2** READER

READING LEVEL
GRADES 1 TO 3

Written by Kathryn Knight

Squirmy and Slimy

Dig into dirt and mud, look under leaves and rocks, and you'll find all kinds of slimy and grubby critters—like earthworms! Who doesn't love these slippery, squirmy soil-makers? They feast on old plant life and turn it into rich soil, helping new plants to grow.

Most earthworms are 4 to 6 inches long. But there are some really big worms lurking out there under your feet. After a good soaky rain, you might see big, plump 10-inch worms on the grass at night. These are nightcrawlers, favorites of fishermen who use them for bait. In Australia, giant Gippsland earthworms can stretch to 9 feet long! But the giant South African earthworm is by far the biggest—reaching 20 feet! That's one big, slimy worm!

Slithery and Slimy

Another slimy backyard guest is the *terrestrial* (land-dwelling) flatworm. These worms range from 2 to 8 inches long and are often colorful. Some look like a piece of string slinking through the garden. They usually stay under leaves and rocks in hot weather or coil into a slime-coated ball. Flatworms are *carnivores* (meat eaters), seeking out earthworms, slugs—and each other!—to eat.

Photo by Shirley Sekarajasingham

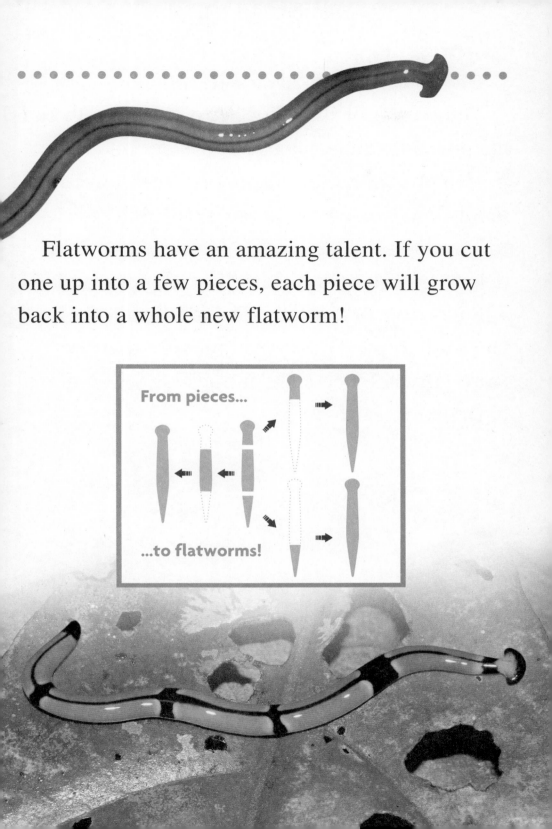

Flatworms have an amazing talent. If you cut one up into a few pieces, each piece will grow back into a whole new flatworm!

From pieces...

...to flatworms!

Slimy Slugs

Those trails of slime you see on your walkway are probably left by slugs. Many slugs munch on garden plants, so they are not often welcome. But these slow-moving critters are really quite fun to watch. They ooze a goopy *mucus* (slime) that helps their soft bodies glide over rough ground.

Slugs have four feelers. The top longer feelers can sense light. The shorter ones are used for smell. If you touch a feeler, the slug will pull it back into its head.

Most slugs are gray or brown, but some are colorful. The big banana slug is yellow. The largest slugs can be 10 to 12 inches long!

UGH!

Frogs, toads, and snakes eat slugs.

Sliding on Slime

Snails are common in most yards. They are much like slugs, but they carry their own shelter around with them. When the sun gets hot, snails can pull into their shells and stay put—which also keeps them safe from hungry animals. Like slugs, snails slowly slide along on slimy mucus.

Snail shells come in many sizes and colors. Many have pretty patterns and stripes. The largest snails are giant African land snails. These can be 10 to 15 inches long!

Slimy Suckers

You may think that blood-sucking leeches only live in water, but there are land leeches, too! These wormlike animals look like flattened slugs—and some like to *eat* worms and slugs. Many have tiny teeth that help them latch on to animals.

A leech's slime helps it stick to its dinner guest. A leech will suck an animal's blood and then drop off to slink away and rest in a shady place.

Slimy and Grubby

Maggots! The very word makes the skin crawl. And when hundreds of these slimy little critters are eating away under the skin of a dead animal, you really *can* see its skin move and "crawl"!

Maggots are young flies. Flies lay eggs on garbage, animal droppings, and *carcasses* (dead bodies). A fly egg hatches into a tiny wormlike creature called a *larva* (**lar**-vah). A fly larva is a maggot. A maggot grows as it feasts on stinky, rotten stuff (which it just *loves*). Next it goes into a *pupa* (**pyu**-pah) stage as it turns into an adult fly. The fly lays more eggs…
more maggots,
maggots, maggots!

Grubby Bugs

If you dig up part of your garden or lawn, you may see some big, soft grubs. Grubs are the larva stage of certain beetles. Most grubs live underground in the dirt munching on plant roots. Other animals, such as moles and lizards, like to munch on grubs. Grubs go into a pupa stage and then emerge from the dirt as adult beetles.

Most grubs will be ½ to 2 inches long. Others grow to be quite large. The grub of some goliath beetles can be 5 inches long! That's a good-size meal for a hungry mole!

Life stages of a chafer beetle

Larva Stage

Pupa Stage

Adult Beetle

Gross and Grubby

Some grubs grow up inside something really gross and grubby—animal *feces* (**fee**-seez), also called dung or poop. Dung beetles feed on this stuff. It's a good thing, too, because it helps rid the land of smelly droppings.

Dung beetles lay eggs in the dung. Some roll chunks of dung into perfect balls, one for each egg. The eggs hatch, and the grubs eat and grow inside the dung. Yum!

Grungy and Grubby

There's one really creepy bug you might not want to find under a rock or leaves. A cockroach! Roaches are quick. If you come across one, it will scurry away on its "hairy" legs. Those spiny hairs help the roach scuttle across any surface, from sand to screen doors, and up your kitchen wall!

Some cockroaches like to live in dirty, filthy places—and they can spread germs wherever they go. So, you may not like seeing roaches while you dig in the dirt, but it's a lot better than seeing them in your house!

YIKES!

A roach can run around for a week without its head!

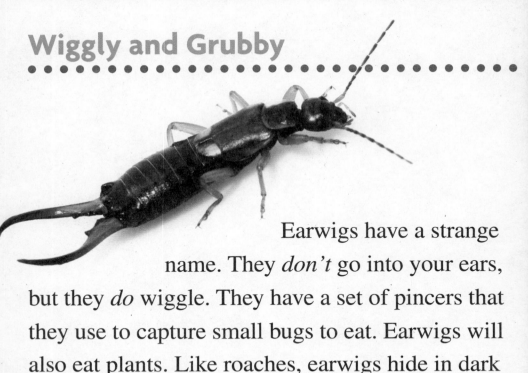

Earwigs have a strange name. They *don't* go into your ears, but they *do* wiggle. They have a set of pincers that they use to capture small bugs to eat. Earwigs will also eat plants. Like roaches, earwigs hide in dark places, such as under rocks and between bricks.

Wriggly and Grubby

The other wiggly, wriggly critters in the dirt are garden centipedes. Centipedes move very quickly. They have 80 to 160 legs! They live in the soil and leaf litter, hunting insects and spiders. They wriggle away with S-shaped movements and are sometimes called "snake centipedes."

Grimy and Grubby

Like centipedes, millipedes have a lot of legs. But these harmless dirt-dwellers eat plants and old leaves and move slowly. They are fun to watch. If you disturb one, it will curl up into a tight coil. The giant African millipede grows to 11 inches. It is often kept as a pet.

Cute and Grubby

There are a lot of strange, creepy, grubby critters in the dirt, but pill bugs are cute. They are not insects. In fact, they are related to shrimp. If you come across them under a log or stone, they may curl up into little balls. They are also called doodlebugs and roly-polies.

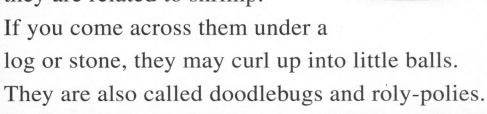

From Slimy to Grubby

You may not see this big, dragonlike bug too often. It's a hellgrammite (**hell-**gruh-mite). It crawls out of its slimy, watery home and looks for a grubby place, like dirt and rotting leaves, to hide. Then this 3-inch creature turns into a fierce dobsonfly.

From worms and grubs to roaches and hellgrammites, just think of the slimy and grubby critters that may be living in your yard!